I'm a Big Sister

A TODDLER PREP™ BOOK

Ready Set Prep

Copyright 2023 ReadySetPrep LLC

Toddler Prep™, ReadySetPrep™, and associated trademarks are owned by and used under license from ReadySetPrep LLC.

All rights reserved. No part of this book may be reproduced or used in any manner without written permission of the copyright owner except for the use of quotations in a book review. For more information, contact author.

All characters and events are products of the author's imagination, and any resemblance to actual events, places or persons, living or dead is entirely coincidental.

Photo credits: © Shutterstock.com

About Toddler Prep™ Books

The best way to prepare a child for any new experience is to help them understand what to expect beforehand, according to experts. And while cute illustrations and fictional dialogue might be entertaining, little ones need a more realistic representation to fully understand and prepare for new experiences.

With Toddler Prep™ Books, a series by ReadySetPrep™, you can help your child make a clear connection between expectation and reality for all of life's exciting new firsts. Born from firsthand experience and based on research from leading developmental psychologists, the series was created by Amy Kathleen Pittman—mom of two who knows (all too well) the value of preparation for toddlers.

You're going to be a big sister -how exciting! Let's talk about what happens when you become a big sister.

Becoming a big sister means that a new baby is joining our family. There will be lots of changes, but lots of fun too.

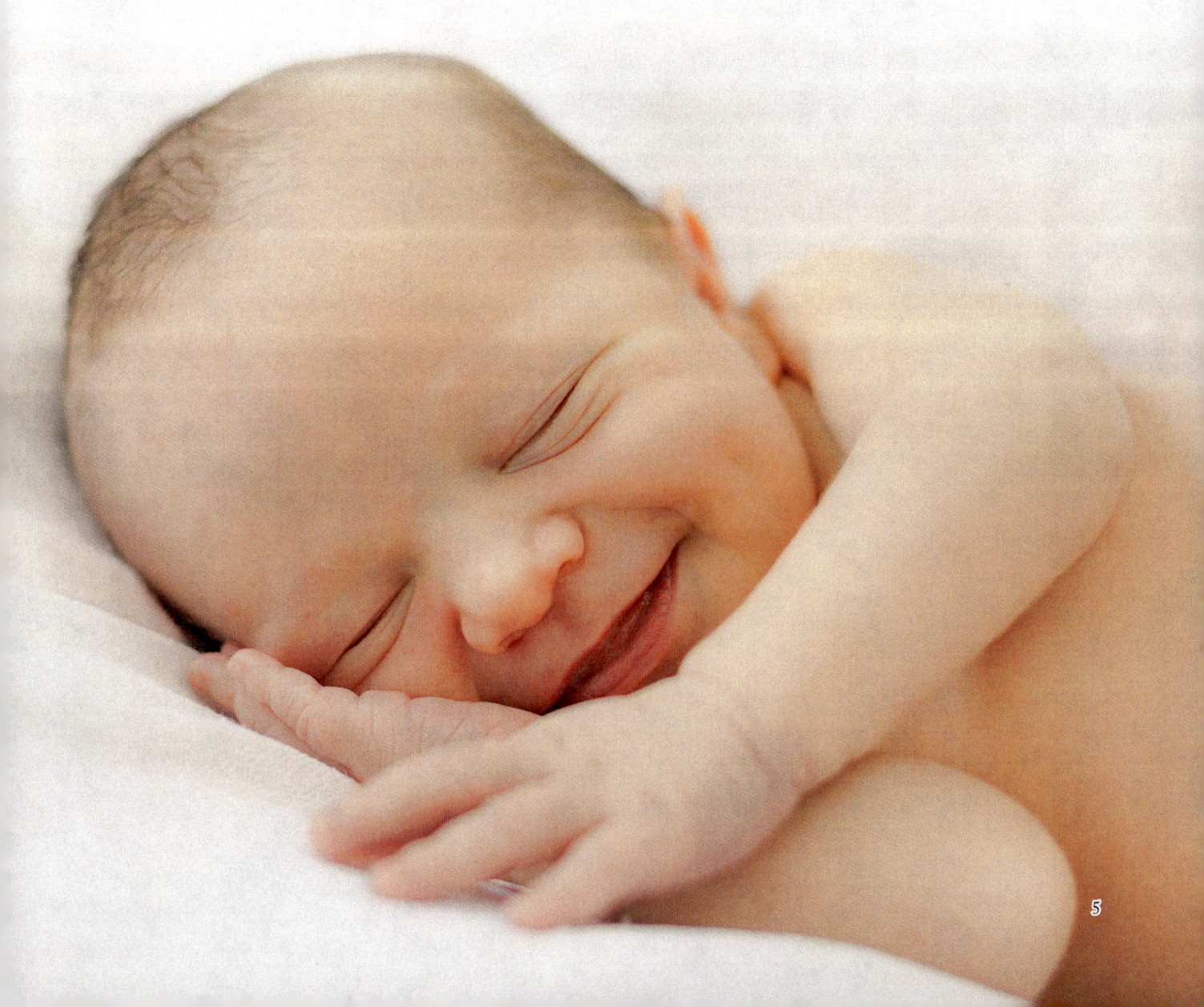

Before the baby arrives, we go to the store to buy all the things that we need.

The baby needs a crib to sleep in, bottles for milk, and lots of diapers.

The baby also needs clothes to wear and toys to snuggle.

At home, we get the baby's room ready. We put together the crib and set up a changing table. Can you help twist the screwdriver?

Then, we wash all their clothes and put them neatly in the drawers.

In the living room, we put a swing in the corner where the baby can sleep and make a spot for extra diapers, too.

Things will be a little different when the baby is here. You might hear the baby cry at night or early in the morning. Babies cry to tell us what they need.

When the baby is sleeping, we play quiet games and use soft voices. Babies need a lot of sleep to grow.

Sometimes, I will be busy taking care of the baby. You may have to wait patiently until I'm done.

There will be lots of fun new things to do after the baby arrives. We will go on walks, and you can help push the stroller.

You will get to cuddle the baby and give them gentle hugs and kisses.

You can also sit on the floor and show them your toys.

Things will be different for a little while, but we will still do all our favorite things together—like play with your toys...

...and go to the playground to see your friends!

And we still get to play games and do silly dances that make us giggle.

When the baby comes, our family will grow bigger, but I will love you just the same.

I will love the new baby AND I will love you, too!

You're going to be such a good big sister!

Made in United States
North Haven, CT
30 October 2023